# And Then the Rain Came

## Edward Ragg

**Cinnamon Press**
:: small miracles from distinctive voices ::

Published by Cinnamon Press
www.cinnamonpress.com

British Library Cataloguing in Publication Data. A CIP record for this book can be obtained from the British Library.

Designed and typeset in Bodoni by Cinnamon Press. Cover design by Adam Craig © Adam Craig.from original artwork: Chinese ideography photo 118953135 © Royer214 | Dreamstime.com

Cinnamon Press is represented by Inpress

# Acknowledgements

Some material from earlier drafts of these poems was adapted for *Arrival at Elsewhere* (Against the Grain Press, 2020), a book-length poem assembled by Carl Griffin with contributions from 100 poets in response to the global pandemic.

'At the Wedding of Water' was inspired by Rachel Brazil's 'The Weirdness of Water' published in *Chemistry World* (Royal Society of Chemistry, April 2020) – also available at:
https://www.chemistryworld.com/features/the-weirdness-of-water/4011260.article

'No Less Us' first appeared as 'COVID-19' on www.edwardragg.com

I would like to thank Jan Fortune, Adam Craig and Cinnamon Press for their origination of this volume and continued support of my work. I would also like to thank Eleanor Goodman, Nazeer Chowdhury, David Tait and Penelope Shuttle.

I especially wish to thank Tan Shu Ying 谭树英 who inspired these poems in numerous ways and for whose friendship I will remain eternally grateful.

Special thanks are also due to Fongyee Walker, whose love and support made the period of isolation in which some of these poems were composed bearable; and who, whatever the weather, sustains me each and every day.

# Contents

## I. And Then the Rain Came

| | |
|---|---|
| And Then the Rain Came | 13 |
| 'I am a child of the Atlantic North…' | 14 |
| Not Only Not Then | 15 |
| Nothing To Be Done | 16 |
| No Will O'The Wisp | 17 |
| Transiting | 18 |
| Of Petrification | 19 |
| Of Petrichor | 20 |
| Of Unexpected Tears | 21 |
| Transatlantic | 22 |
| Returning Alien | 23 |
| Untimely | 24 |
| No Time Like the Present | 25 |

## II. Present Future Perfect

| | |
|---|---|
| Anna Livia | 28 |
| At the Wedding of Water | 30 |
| No Less Us | 32 |
| Enough | 33 |
| Enough is Enough | 34 |
| Albaldah by Night | 36 |
| For True Love Waits | 37 |
| Bridge at the Wetlands of Tongli | 38 |
| The Clarity of Water | 40 |
| Mr Pickwick Presents | 42 |
| The Garden | 44 |
| Lacrima | 45 |
| Political Poem 2.0 | 46 |

# And Then the Rain Came

*When the rain came to wet me once, and the wind to make me chatter; when the thunder would not peace at my bidding, there I found 'em, there I smelt 'em out.*

~ King Lear, *The Tragedy of King Lear*

*Fresh, clean water cannot be taken for granted. And it is not – water is political, and litigious.*

~ Dr Michael Burry

'Present'

Noun 1: the present time; the present tense of a language.

Noun 2: something presented, a gift.

Adjective: now existing or in progress; being in view or under consideration; constituting the one actually involved; in existence at the moment an utterance is spoken or written; being in a specified place; of, relating to, or constituting a verb tense expressive of present time or the time of speaking; (*archaic*) instant, immediate; (*obsolete*) attentive, mentally alert.

Verb: to make a gift of; to bestow formally; to nominate to a beneficiary; to bring to one's attention; to bring before the public; to introduce socially; to bring a formal public charge against; to aim or direct (esp. a weapon).

Etym. Middle English, via Old French: from Latin *praesent* ('being at hand'), present participle of *praeesse*, from *prae* 'before' + *esse* 'to be'.

*This book is dedicated to the remarkable properties of water*

# I. And Then the Rain Came

## And Then the Rain Came

Frost thawed to dew in the sparkling garden.
It was late winter acknowledging spring.
Birds returned to song. And then the rain came.
Great Atlantic gusts battering shrubbery
and the compliant trees. There was then
a temptation to conceive a mind in spring.
A mind weathering that weather there and then.
There is a temptation. No sooner thought
than metaphor drenched that garden.
I have lived in the various elements of this earth,
but not the quick. Mine no mind admitting
water: its shaping spirit and replenishing gifts.
So the metaphor dried. The withered snowdrops
and precocious daffodils blew in that light.
Dew evaporated to a new day, which flowed.

# 'I am a child of the Atlantic North…'

*And I was saved by northern light*

*~ Saint Saviour*

I am a child of the Atlantic North,
of slate-grey clouds and slanting rain.
I am that child. Heading west, emerging
from thickets drenched onto sand-caked
beaches soaked with saline spray.
Mollusc-aerosol moistening the bearded
lichen that clings to every rock, conjuring
mussels and labia. Creased-up smiles,
affection of the gruff phrase, my ear cocked
to heartfelt taunts as frequent as rain.
And then? Love and China. From Beijing
to the furnaces of Chongqing. Not born of it.
The women of Chongqing fearless and white.
Thus I cling to the cool firm of Atlantic rock,
if not saved by the distal, the northern light.

# Not Only Not Then

Not by light was I saved, not only, not then.
*Not only not then* but once years of rain
shaped the inviting earth before all talk
of saviours, even salvation, drained away.
Instead, there was the odour, the fragrance
of rain. This rain here redolent of that place
there where childhood, its damp English houses,
mould, wet towels and dripping hair,
the cat squirming, the dog shaking her coat,
expectant, obedient as that child, there each
neuron-clapped cloud flashed with memory.
Across the valley I watched that weather spread:
forgot its smell, staring over the farthest hill.
Unaware olfactory ghosts were nosing
the smouldering synapses of what we were.

# Nothing To Be Done

What are we to do about yearning?
Yearning, desire: which are not the same.
Yearning after desire. Rain spreads
across the windowpane. How many
hours have I lost to this? Another's desire.
She feels for me in the Shanghai night
as I observe this Durham afternoon
feeling her. Nothing to be done:
which is not the same as doing nothing
or saying 'We can do nothing, my love'.
We can. Rain percussive on tiles and panes.
Yearning is that desire which can
never be answered... Do not answer, love.
Nothing to be done. Love (persistently) quiet.
How the light rain of my desire falls all night.

# No Will O'The Wisp

Cirrostratus dabbing the blue sky
above ample-bellied altocumulus like
the peachy flesh of Enlightenment divines.
Or the sturdiest Tang women shadowing
the earth on saddleback. Each looking
up – or are they? – at the wispiest lines
of natural elevation. I must... get out.
Gloved and masked. The light on the lawn
last night inexplicable. No cloud explains.
Lends no other name to folklore than
what each becomes. Meteorological,
perhaps. *Very like a whale* but...
nameless. Not one noun between them.
This will, like others, pass. Go.
New clouds come, heralding rain.

# Transiting

Cambered roads of the wet zones.
Showers shimmering across distant lochs.
Rainbows fading in the heather light.
Then, on to cities, they say, built for rain.
Pouring millions into levees, saturating
minds with the sirens of reliable defence.
In Guangzhou every plane grounds.
Rain lashes the sweltering earth,
the air dank with five-spice and graft.
Nothing here but the present. Even as
the city contemplates its sinking horizons.
Joy of acceptance as one stranded without
a drop of fear. Fierce energy of weather
as nothing else. So we move on, save those,
like Sisyphus, rolling perpetual stones.

# Of Petrification

Stone-roller? Consider how it is always
to a perpetual present of punishment
for past acts the grand myths commit us.
So the mind ossifies, pondering only
the certain past and its painful future.
Such punishment for thought and deed.
For thought indeed... No rain simply
by falling awakens to here the mind
petrified by everything but the present.
Medusa is the past because her face is
your future. By that atlas of pain lies another.
You. But she was the victim, not monster.
Raped by Poseidon, Athena struck gorgon.
When I look into her eyes, speak of the rain
wetting our cheeks, snakes fall from her hair.

## Of Petrichor

Once the snakes fell from her hair,
she awoke to rain dappling her
singed eyebrows and shining cheeks.
We laughed at the word *petrichor*.
An etymologist's wet dream.
Medusa said she'd understood a thing
or two about divine fluids and stone.
Its grating consonantal sound and
uninviting vowels. Only that terminal *or*
conjuring after-thoughts of the rising odour
of wet earth after rain. Precise *petrichor*
still ensnared in its verbal roots once
the sodden aromas of all places fade away.
Involatile, trapped in Sisyphus's stone.
Or a dictionary's leaves moulding with rain.

## Of Unexpected Tears

Every year the bush burned.
Gumtrees carbonised to treacle resin.
Dams dried, pools plastered with leaves.
Saline striations flowered the cracked earth
as hoses frayed. Children of a dry country
learn the husky language of dust and haze.
Every sunset at the horizon beige.
The insistent magic of water conjures
its startling brightness in a table jug or
shallow bath flickering in the dying light.
At the Victorian kindergarten playtime
fell to tears and sudden darts inside.
Not a drop of rain in eight years. They cried
in the floodgate of signifier and signified.
The teachers' eyes wet with excitation.

# Transatlantic

I hid from the so very English satisfactions.
The superior countryside, the climate sensibly
moderate, lamenting rain. Their draining
*changeable*. Even feeling oddly disappointed
at prolonged sun. An American poet says:
*You and the poem are dancing together.*
*Don't tell your partner what to believe.*
Rain falls again. The English Channel
contends with Atlantic gales. I laugh
at imagined disdain as each droplet
wets my changeable face. Not the word
rain in a poem falling onto the page
precisely where we'd thought, but water echoing.
As it is: off cobbled streets and sodden brick.
Over there they say things differently they say.

# Returning Alien

Durham Cathedral darkens with rain.
The A1 awash at the deserted airport hotel.
Morning clouds swirl dense blacks of grey.
Then Newcastle-Paris, Paris-Tianjin.
The tarmac arid, our suitcases evaporating
disinfectant spray. Hazmat suits interview,
test and convey all subjects to quarantine.
It is a relief to be seen in Chinese eyes again.
No stranger to anyone than any returning alien.
Weeks from now I will touch the ground
in the Yinchuan dust and take your hand.
Dense Cabernet and cumin-scented lamb.
Faces flayed with wind and the Ningxia
dirt gritting our teeth as we try to kiss.
How humid the hearts in these desert hills.

## Untimely

The Beijing sky is orange-yellow-grey.
Layers of dust and fine sand powder
the concrete plazas, the pavements snaking
like faraway dunes sculpted by wind. I sift
between one hand and another heart time
falling through an hourglass. My own heart
inverted. Watching each grain of sand
descend through the tight neck as outside
Gobi grit defines the advancing hours.
Is time lost to us? Or the world merely ahead?
Heavy dusts of mind clear with sleep or
attention to the sensation of sand in our palms.
But the heart... flowing like that storm which
dazzled the garden with gratitude. May the heart
be late? Our ribcages touch, longing for rain.

# No Time Like the Present

There is no time like the present
because the present is no time.
Now is then, if described.
Thus, it is preferable *to avoid
description.* (Really? *Best avoided.*)
But the poem is here. *After the fact.*
No, here. We are here. *Yes, I see that
now.* And, while here, always describes
the scene a little before we arrived.
In the topography of inherited sounds.
Not fact exactly, but the pre-sent present.
As an old voice, still quick, quickens
to verb, pure verb. Shucking oysters,
salivating brine, anticipating mouths
of cool saline wine. Happening on

participles.

# II. Present Future Perfect

## Anna Livia

Joyce saunters   by the waters                 of the Seine

            to hear her      engushing                and engurgling

then
            in the labials
                        of Anna Livia Plurabelle...
                                                Allaluyah ...

He smiles
                when      his cane
                                    taps      the cobbles

            iridescent            as flickering
                                    fish scales        lit

with sunsetting
                        oils          of      water-coloured                rain

            and hums        to his lips
                                    in lilting
                                                tenor
                                                    the light

of her                  lost   Liffey
                                alluvial Anna
                                                    Alivia
            alla pluribus        this   beau 'n belle
                                            letting on

at last    because    she says
                                and doesn't   mind      a-sayin it
            how    every telling   is    a taling

                                                    though
the telling

is

present

                and presents      this   spindly   oddity
                                                of a man

murmuring  of   Ireland sober        and   Ireland        stiff

28

       and    Paris
                  in

the half-light

     now    in

          the forgotten   Chasselas  of his repairing    gait
muttering     some prayer  of     thanks
                      O Momma Shawl Weaver!

Patroness of his her their
                verbal     excess

   by Penelope's

          needle         and         thread

   unravelling...

to begin   again         once   more      and

now
    how Anna flows
               and is
                    flowing   and flowing is

his Anna Lifting
         her   banks
             all
                spread    as
                      she
                        comes
    for she is
           coming
               yes
                her waters   engushing

and
        washing
           all
               over
                 him         forever

    riverrun    everyone riverrunning her   O   Anna
                      yes

## At the Wedding of Water

The Stockholm chemist
considers the remarkable

properties of water.
Chill and like other liquids

it grows denser
*unless colder than -4C.*

Freeze and its icy
capillaries form so

cautiously you can watch
its *fluid motion to -41C.*

The chemist drinks tea and
thinks: 'Is it one liquid or two?'

Two liquids kissing
in their shifting embrace,

flaunting *so many hydrogen
bonds* for *such a small*

molecule
...

Its glassy state, the *no man's land*
where none sees its liquid phase.

The chemist wonders: 'Perhaps
they are like guests at a wedding'.

High density sat at tables
listening to the band,

watching low density
fling themselves around.

Water from the Old English
*wæter* soaked in Russian's

*voda* riding on the crest of
*unda* wave on Latinate wave.

Stockholm looks like rain...


No chemist truly leaves
the laboratory the same.

The droplets touching
the pavement *so ordered*

though they rose
from rivers and sea.

She will take her bath tonight
and stare into the water

thinking of the icy-blue
eyes of the man in the band

who caught her glance
as she rose from her chair

that covalent evening
flowing

in his direction...

## No Less Us

How can I say, my love, the days
denied us have been nothing to us?

I walk where you have walked.
And you watch me wherever I go.

Your videoed smile, livestreams
of the best of us, a casual ice-cream

on a pier where my shadow does not
fall, as yours may never cross,

though its virtual touch runs through
my body running along the shore.

These are no less us than the lips
that defined our every kiss.

Devices they worried would halt
our lives, holding them on ice

in a faraway bay all glistening and
white, have kept us alive. Kept us all.

My love, you may not touch my hand,
but your palms surround my heart

in its febrile beat seeking your heat.
The ear in the dark knows

the temperature of our love,
if not situation. Check it by daylight

and it'll clock the same, outside
numbers and fever and pain.

Were we never to kiss again
I would hold you in our heart:

our heart of hearts. You
no girl of memory, me

no less your
breathing soul.

# Enough

Rain falls all night.

There is no determination.

Only for the listening heart.

By morning the windows
gleam bright frames of gold.

Swallows dart and weave
across the low grass

in efficient arcs
feeding on the hour.

So the listening
heart remembers

providence
is quiet

and can watch.

# Enough is Enough

Its excess was enough. From an English classroom,
as the Berlin Wall fell, Blake's *Proverbs of Hell*
read in an uncertain voice all the proverbial
uncrooked path to *Enough! or Too Much.*
Which sounded like a question, then.
But, later, an equivalence where contraries
were equally true. Though in the devil's voice
any teenager could tell were really just
the same (if you felt like it). That was when
I listened attentively to what could never
suffice, as they asked for more, more.
Berlin's past was in our history books
before the cascading screens of the future.
The news broadcast *Tonight, we present
the situation in Berlin.* For homework I read
again *Dip him in the river who loves water.*
And he will not drown? Perhaps he dies
happily in that element. (Dip not plunge.
Water does not equal death, my friend).
In Germany there were new immersions
of frustration and delight. As if a crowd
gathered by a diviner's rod. But England
was already going, going, gone, as I
too wanted more. But not of England.
Not its endearing understatements. Nor even
Albion slumbering under London's streets.
I turn to my school dictionary now and scan
*Present. Adj. [...] (archaic)* attentive.
Why did I hide, then, when poetry
already showed love's doorway to life
is the same doorway everywhere?
Each portal a discovery. The present world
*closed to the senses five* for a moment
presents. Unseen, unheard, untouched,
sans odour, sans taste. Enough. As if
we had already sent ahead for word
of ourselves arriving. They taught us tautologies
as they tried to teach Blake. Enough is enough.
He saw the face of God at four. Not by the hour.

Knowing *of wisdom no clock can measure.*
Unchained from an Enlightenment pocket watch.
Enough. For who may gauge the scale of miracle?
These senses insatiable to life contain
no contentment for the unpresent mind.
I seek no eternity, not even what lies beyond
these fallen walls, or the clock ticking, or the taste
of your absent lips, not what my hand cannot touch,
except the overwhelmingly, excessively enough.

## Albaldah by Night

I sit by the window
of the old house.

It is no longer raining.

A single star shines
in the clear night.

Wondering if ignorance
has its charm. Or is it

innocence unplotted
in the constellated mind?

But Albaldah shines
after our inquiries.

Mass of six suns five
hundred light years away.

How reassuring to be dwarfed.
Being ourselves small miracles.

Star gazers cast their eyes
on this sight in search of Pluto.

So it is in the galaxies
of words seeking smaller

almost indetectable sounds
pulled by silence.

Beneath those the ever
tinier universes love shows.

# For True Love Waits

I thought we were divided
by cities and rival Chinas
and provinces winning prizes
in the pageants of distant islands

where the pines are always pining
and the cartographer maps out
silence or by each slope's gradient
draws the yearning of each sunrise.

In your city, the traffic halts
for pedestrians. The pathways
filter rain, each slab of pavement
spirit-levelled the same.

In my city, the lorries, cars and bikes
show passing acquaintance with lights
and brushing familiarity with walkers.
But by these we are not divided.

You say love is not chasing but waiting.
I am waiting in traffic, again.
Not for a single moment the same
the waiting heart beats the same.

Love is not the residuum of absence,
but what remains after you have gone.
And what we shared as our breaths
mingled in the smaller hours,

which, though now by memory
caressed, whispers in our ears and
lays out the very horizon before us...

Love is not the sun at its zenith
but the horizon at that ocean's edge.
No dramatic apex but the hand that takes
yours at each station of each journey

changing places in every waiting room.

## Bridge at the Wetlands of Tongli

We drove from Shanghai that winter's day
in English weather talking of clouds and rain,
as the sun broke through the humid air
still moistening our lips, thirsting
for the wetlands of Tongli.

In the deep shade of camphor trees and
swaying bamboo, we are maskless and free.
You walk by my side. I watch you smile
considering each character of your name.
Your *deep pool* reflecting *tree flowers*
as we take a boat through the green water
of the marshes. Then walk back through
groves of peach and pear that will,
later this year, blossom and fructify,
their roots holding firm beneath the earthen
water channels so precisely carved.

Last summer I dreamt of this bridge unseen.
But the water was deeper and surging
with tidal waves no swimmer would brave.
Immense darkness of water. Like the black
shades at the bottom of a glass, in the dregs
of a bottle. That was when I longed to touch
the lowest layers of that riverbed.

Water girl of the water towns...

A lazier poet would call you water nymph,
reclining on a worn bench with dusty scrolls
and bamboo scripts. Or dream of you,
within his notes, until human voices wake us.
He hides in Li Bai's cloak or out-Ophelias
Ophelia caressing the inevitable garlands.
As one incapable of his own distress,
he drowns. I will not follow him.

Was it really this bridge before me
in the darker hours of an English night?
You walk ahead as I stop fast
recollecting the traditional arch and
greystone columns now fixed before us.
Your voice flows through my listening heart.
The water is motionless at last.
How easy it is to take your hand
without hesitation, without guilt.

Water girl of the water towns...

# The Clarity of Water

*Life seems wonderfully clear and simple in a boat 2ft x 15ft,*
*powered by me and the whim of the sea.*

~ *Tedman Littwin, teacher.*

I

Each summer you and your family
wound down from Deerfield, Mass,

to build kayaks on Connecticut sand.
Across the sound, Long Island a line

against your beach house not always
visible between paint pots and books,

wood sheaves and polymer. Perhaps
you considered Whitman or O'Hara

as you coaxed the kayak to water,
paddle-tight. But I reckon your mind

leant on the elemental Atlantic, riding
or chopping in measure of the sea.

At once alone, at once bobbing
the crest of family, the schoolyard

hardly many, if any, waves away.
How a boat feels cutting blue water.

## II

Here at Longqing gorge winter water
is flowing ice: one crystalline waterfall

almost as arid as the Badaling rock.
No pasture here and Beijing a few

smoke-signals from the Great Wall's
undulating watch. *Clear and simple.*

A frozen river miles from the weight
of ocean and leagues from New England,

I fancy your craft would cleave
the winter air well enough, river-dragon.

The sea's density is so many walls
delineating earth's clarity.

Now your timber is at sea... But your
voice cuts water like never before.

The paddle's blade an axiom.
Your words pacific, swelling, ice-clear.

## Mr Pickwick Presents

His papers no longer undisclosed.
Presented to the world in glittering
instalments. Interwoven with Pickwick's
proceedings, yarn upon polished yarn.
As a novelist extends his practising hand.

Each of his confederates stumbling
on the narrative of the hour. Divulged
from the moist lips of a travelling tinker
emboldened by brandy and water.
Everything fascinating to him, as
Pickwick sloughs off the chrysalis
of caricature to fluttering man.

The dissolution of his society.
The Pickwick Club gone:
no more nit-picking minutes
or punch-drunk protestations.

We see him in his retirement.
The final house, neat, compact, elegant
but not unlived. As this tale of tales
concludes – the expected denouement,
with all but Pickwick paired – he
whispers in Dickens's late-burning ear

*Let us present.*

So Dickens writes *And in the midst
of all this, stood Mr. Pickwick,
his countenance lighted up with smiles...*
pauses, looks up from the page and smiles.

Then Dickens writes *Breakfast is announced*
as he presently leads everyone to table.

*Mr. Pickwick... pauses for an instant,*
*and looks round him. As he does so,*
*the tears roll down his cheeks*
*in the fulness of his joy.*

So Pickwick in perpetuity presents.
Like the figures of Keats's urn.

*Let us leave our old friend in one of those*
*moments of unmixed happiness, of which,*
*if we seek them, there are ever some,*
*to cheer our transitory existence here...*

His tears of joy definitive rain.

# The Garden

There is movement in the garden.
Lear sees. He is quieter now.
Sat on a bench with a cloak tracing
the outline of his crownless head.
May a king be uncrowned? He reflects.
Deposed, perhaps, but he recalls
his own coronation. All the gardens
festooned and garlanded in light.
He reflects. How the garden resembles
King Hamlet's resting place.
No one approaches. But in the safety
of the word we may sit with him and
listen awhile. Like a monarch who
watches from the corner of one eye.
In the porches of his ears no poison
poured but what is said. Was that
his voice moving across the border?
He smiles at the scene. The ungrateful
daughters might have stooped at nothing
to attain his end being theirs. If he be
nothing, they'd take dominion everywhere.
But he smelt them out. How nature serves
us best. Winter comes. Though there is
movement, with the frozen shrubbery
he will not contend. To the defiant bushes
he will not dictate. They are implacable.
The clouds above, all the sovereign elements
he never gave kingdom, he accepts.
As the winds of heaven caress
his bearded face. So fortune fits.
His cheeks furrow with water
in skin-indented rivulets. *For the rain
it raineth every day*. For the man of rain
it rains no less. But there is movement.

# Lacrima

In certain sepulchres were found vessels
where once mourners' tears were thought
to be buried with the deceased. Blown glass
lipping the meniscus's edge. *Lacrimatoria*
brimming with Roman grief. Whether tears
or balms, the blown glass supplemented
each obligatory obol with transparent face.

Today, my forefinger and thumb clench
the stem of another glass levelled with wine.
Unfined, unfiltered, shimmering opaquely
in the unburied sheen of late afternoon.
The suspended aromas and granular tannins
of a life's endeavours expressed in time.

Its present future perfect unspoken. As it is.
Where we will have had, where we will have been.
The Roman mourners, the vigneron walking home.
To initial lives. Until the first odour uncorked.
Singing its fading song in my afternoon hand.
The present retrospective of a single year
crossing the river between life and memory.

As the world burns... From North Coast
to New South Wales. Howell Mountain
to Hunter. Glass fire to cindered gum.
The stench of smoke-infused grapes left
hanging in the exact and furious wind.

Those who work this land, the soil in their hands,
who plucked, crushed, vinified, and pressed
their clustered hearts hastily packing
valuables into a boiling car at night.
Angular torchlight pruning the heads
of mountain trees in the shadows of flames.
In the flames of flames.

So many destemmed, deracinated souls.
So many. And the tears, the tears:
how they keep flaring inextinguishable.

# Political Poem 2.0

I

A quality of light,
of waves or

the sound of water
(whichever the

less abstract)
in tin cans or

dry pails
dreaming,

is the shadow
or quality of

objects moving
before that light.

Darkening shadows
if not clouds

heavy with rain
spreading across

the cracked earth

dreaming...

## II

The clarity of water
is as nothing

to the cleanliness,
your Honour.

Though each may
settle, may be settled

by increasingly
volatile measures.

Whose water is this?
Is it potable?

The earth decides.

The earth does not.

Does not speak
of water rights,

of wells drying,
of crystal salts.

III

He speaks of
the quality of water.

*Look how clear*
sound the vowels

and crystalline
consonants.

His utterance
saline.

IV

We are parched:
our voices husky,

our tongues smarting,
our lips cracked.

The only orator
is the best orator.

(She has a glass
of water to hand).

## V

A white man on a desert road.
White men on desert roads.

Everyone of all colours
walking on desert roads.

Above them satellites map
evaporation rates,

the growth of algae,
the etc. etc. &c.

VI

Perhaps I was, then,
rising in my powers;

and, having risen,
could not escape.

I say poetry is
not escapism.

But I had not yet
understood how

to sit at a table and
drink a glass of water,

gratefully,
watching clouds pass.

VII

We are wary of poems
that announce things

and wary of those
that cannot.

Not wavering
into language.

Not wavering
in it.

## VIII

Desert hawk,
they say you are

master surveyor
among the thermals.

For you know
there is neither

beauty nor play
without sustenance,

and nothing, truly
nothing

without water.

## IX

And then
the rain came.

The farmer leapt
from her bed.

One said for forty
nights and forty days

it would surely rain.
Another *Go to hell*.

Another
*Why, we are on our way...*

All inundated.

The earth requiring
no Noah of

the new verses
and nothing of us.

Not then, not now.

No Noah of
the new verses.

And then
the rain came.